30

Keys To A Successful Life

KEVIN A TREASURE

30 KEYS TO A SUCCESSFUL LIFE
Copyright © 2014 by Decisions Determine Destiny Press

Decisions Determine Destiny Press

Ordering Information:
Quantity sales. Special discounts are available on quantity purchases by corporations, associations, and others. For details, contact the publisher at the address above.

Orders by U.K. trade bookstores and wholesalers. Please contact Kevin Treasure:

Mob: 07903 940 399
Email: kevintreasure@gmail.com
Website: www.kevintreasure.com
Copyright © 2014 – Kevin A. Treasure

Edited by: Sherma Xavier-Walcott
Printed in the United Kingdom

First Edition 2014

ISBN: 978-0-9927831-1-2

Dedication
To my beautiful wife Michelle and my children,
Kevelle, Keturah and Kezzia.

TABLE OF CONTENTS

INTRODUCTION

Success
noun
[mass noun]

1 the accomplishment of an aim or purpose:
   *the president had some **success in** restoring confidence*

* the attainment of fame, wealth, or social status:
   the success of his play

* *[count noun]* a person or thing that achieves desired aims or attains fame, wealth, etc.
   *To judge from league tables, the school is a success, I must **make a success of** my business*

Are you ready to attain the Success you have been dreaming of? The keys are proven, the quotes are inspiring.

Applying these can make the world of difference.

Take Action and Change the World.

Kevin Treasure

1

REALISATION

Admit you need to change.
You don't like where you are
and you need to change.
Success starts with a
made up mind.

Do not remember the former things, Nor consider
the things of old. Behold, I will do a new thing.
– Isaiah 43:18-19 –

2

DETERMINE

What true success means to you, Is it a happy marriage, security, fulfilled goals. Lots of money does not always equal success.

I've never chased money. It's always been about what I can do to motivate and inspire people.
– Tyler Perry –

3

BELIEF

Believe you can, if you don't believe you will succeed, you won't. Success starts in the mind, if your mind is messed up; your life will be messed up, what a person believes is what they will eventually become. What happens in your mind will happen in time.

The only place where your dream becomes impossible is in your own thinking.
– Robert H Schuller –

4

GOALS

*Set a goal and stick to it, do
not attempt too many things,
Choose goal and finish it and
move on to the next project,
Give it 100%. Attempting to do
too many things at the same
time is sometimes the
downfall of many.*

*Don't set your goals too low. If you don't need
much, you won't become much.*
– Jim Rohn –

5

MISTAKES

Stop complaining about your mistakes; they are in the past, quit complaining and start learning from them, mistakes can sometimes be the launch pad to your greatest achievements. Don't cry over mistakes, learn from them.

It's fine to celebrate success but it is more important to heed the lessons of failure.
– Bill Gates –

6

STUDY

Read and learn about successful people, how they made it, what they did, what they overcame. Gain as much knowledge as possible and never stop learning.

And that ye study to be quiet, and to do your own business, and to work with your own hands, as we commanded you.
– 1st Thessalonians 4:11 –

7

EVALUATE

Evaluate what you really need to do, stop wasting time on people and things that are going nowhere.

Evaluate the people in your life, then promote, demote or terminate. Evaluation will usually provoke change.

8

PASSION

Do what you love, you are not going to be happy in this life unless you are doing something you love doing. If what you are doing does not have your heart, there will be no real drive to complete it.

Find your passion, and it's no longer work.
— L A Ried —

9

GIFTING

Find your gifting/talent and use it to generate your income, you will find you'll be getting paid for something you love doing.

A man's gift makes room for him,
And brings him before great men.
– Proverbs 18:16 –

10

EXPERT

Become an expert in your field, you should know your chosen field more than anyone else.

Give Another What He Cannot Find Anywhere Else And He Will Keep Returning.
– Mike Murdock –

11

PERSISTENCE

*Be persistent in what you do.
Do not procrastinate. Keep
going forward. If one door
shuts, search for another.*

*Don't quit, Suffer now and live the rest
of your life as a champion.*
– Muhammad Ali –

12

PROBLEM SOLVING

Find a problem and solve it,
you'll be sought after when
you become recognised
for solving problems.

When you focus on problems you'll have
more problems, when you focus on possibilities
you'll have more opportunities.
– Unknown –

13

TIME

Be prepared to put in time, Success will not happen overnight. Don't waste time, Time is valuable, use it wisely.

There are seven days in a week, and 'Someday' isn't one of them.
– Dr O'Neal –

14

ASK

Ask questions, questions, questions, questions, you don't know everything; someone has the answers to the thing you don't know.

Ask, and it will be given to you; seek, and you will find; knock, and it will be opened to you.
– Jesus –

15

SACRIFICE

Be prepared to make some sacrifices, you may have to stay up a bit later, cancel some nights out, turn down some parties, a small price to pay to gain what you really want.

In Life, you don't get anywhere or do anything you hope to without some sort of sacrifice.
– Stephen Saad –

16

RISK

Be prepared to take risks, you will have to take some risk, you may have to trust people, you would not normally trust, go places you would not normally go. Some people call it a gamble, some will call it faith.

The biggest risk is not taking any risk... In a world that is changing really quickly, the only strategy that is guaranteed to fail is not taking risks.
– Mark Zuckerberg –

17

MISUNDERSTOOD

Be prepared to be misunderstood, not everyone is going to understand why you do what you do. But if you have a goal and you know where you are going, everyone does not need to understand. Just do it.

Don't let the noise of others' opinions drown out your own inner voice. And most important, have the courage to follow your heart and intuition.
– Steve Jobs –

18

REPUTATION

Treat people the way you would want to be treated, put yourself in your customers shoes, as you go along in this journey of success remember you are also building your reputation. Your reputation can make you or destroy you.

A good name is to be chosen rather than great riches.
– Proverbs 22:1 –

19

COMPARISON

Never compare yourself to others; keeping up with the Jones will usually lead to a life of un-fulfilment. There is only one you, you are an original, and no one can do what you do. There has never been another you and there will never ever be another you. You are unique.

If you don't stick to your values when they're being tested, they're not values: they're hobbies.
– Jon Stewart –

20

FOCUS

*Learn to say no to things that
will distract you. Many people
have great ideas, quick money
schemes, which may be good,
but if your heart is not in it,
it will distract you from
what you love doing.*

The Only Reason Men Fail is Broken Focus.
– Mike Murdock –

21

FAMILY

Keep your loved ones informed of everything you are doing, they are important to you, their happiness is also important. You do not want to achieve your goals and then find out your wife wants to leave you and your children no longer know you because you have neglected them in your race for success.

There is no doubt that it is around the family and the home that all the greatest virtues, the most dominating virtues of humans, are created, strengthened and maintained.
– Winston Churchill –

23

22

INTEGRITY

Never compromise your integrity. It is too valuable an asset to lose. You will be known for what you stand for.

Our true character is what we become when no one is watching.
– Unknown –

23

MOTIVATION

Do whatever it takes to stay motivated, some people are motivated by hearing their favourite speaker, or sitting by the lake, a walk in the park. Do whatever it takes to get motivated and stay motivated.

Successful and unsuccessful people do not vary greatly in their abilities. They vary in their desires to reach their potential.
– John Maxwell –

24

NETWORK

Learn to network with all kinds of people, from all kinds of backgrounds. Build up a file of people who can help you achieve your goal.

If you want to go fast, go alone.
If you want to go far, go with others.
– African Proverb –

25

APPEARANCE

Always look the part people will see you before they hear you, but never judge others by their appearance, don't judge every book by its cover. Everyone you meet won't all come in the packaging you're expecting.

What lies behind appearance is usually another appearance.
– Mason Cooley –

26

BUDGET

Know your budget; you can accomplish great things if you budget right and spend wisely.

A budget is telling your money where to go instead of wondering where it went.
– Dave Ramsey –

27

DEBT

If you've made up your mind to be successful you should of already made up your mind to be debt free. Become an enemy to debt.

The rich rules over the poor, and the borrower is the slave of the lender.
– Proverbs 22:7 –

28

REST

Learn to take a break when it's needed. Some people spend half their life killing themselves to gain success and then the other half of their life trying to recover from the journey.

Take my yoke upon you, and learn of me; for I am meek and lowly in heart; and you shall find rest for your soul.
– Jesus –

29

ENJOY

Enjoy the journey, have fun on the way to where you are going. Enjoy the process.

The dream I chased took me on a journey,
A journey more rewarding than the goals.
– Shah Rukh Khan –

30

SEEK

Seek God's guidance in everything you do. Put him first and ask him for direction, he will order your steps.

Trust in the Lord with all your heart and lean not unto your own understanding, In all your ways acknowledge him and he shall direct thy path.
– King Solomon –

THE POWER OF
DIVINE
DIRECTION

The Winners Mentality *Series*

KEVIN A TREASURE

COMING SOON

Kevin A. Treasure

DECISIONS
DETERMINE
DESTINY:

Stories and Scenarios

The Decisions You Make Today, Determine Where You'll Be Tomorrow

GIMM RADIO

For the best in gospel music, preaching and teaching.
http://www.gimmradio.com
http://www.gimm.tv

www.ingramcontent.com/pod-product-compliance
Lightning Source LLC
Chambersburg PA
CBHW060631030426
42337CB00018B/3297